FACEBOOK

ADVERTISING

Crack the Facebook Ad code with an easy-to-implement Facebook marketing plan that really works and reach 4000 potential customers every month

TABLE OF CONTENT

CHAPTER 1: FACEBOOK ADS 5

CHAPTER 2: WHY AND HOW TO CREATE A FAN PAGE? 19

CHAPTER 3: INSTALL FACEBOOK PIXELS....................................25

CHAPTER 4: HOW TO ADVERTISE ON FACEBOOK 32

CHAPTER 5: FIVE DIFFERENT AUDIENCES YOU CAN REACH 43

CHAPTER 6: LANDING PAGES AND FACEBOOK ADS 50

CHAPTER 7: SIDE-SCROLLING CAROUSEL ADS........................54

CHAPTER 8: FACEBOOK ADS AND COPYWRITING 56

CHAPTER 9: HOW TO REDUCE COSTS ON FACEBOOK 59

CHAPTER 10: SPLIT TEST AND MULTIPLE ADS IN FEW SECONDS...66

CHAPTER 11: GET BETTER RESULTS SPYING COMPETITORS 74

CONCLUSIONS..80

CHAPTER 1: FACEBOOK ADS

With the hundreds of millions of Facebook users that are logged on daily to the net, this attracted the attention of most web marketers, and they are taking advantage of this scenario.

It is a very good decision for web marketers to place advertisements on Facebook because of its vast potential to reach out to several thousands of potential customers.

But it is important to note that Facebook has very strict guidelines which you have to adhere to, and doing otherwise will not get your ads accepted on this social site.

Acceptance of your ads in Facebook will be the first step to making your ads on this social site and can make you attain the success of your web business. If you have plenty of products in your line, you have only to choose the ideal and the best product to be promoted on Facebook.

Remember that users on Facebook are not there to even think of buying, and you don't have to make them feel suffocated with all your product lines poured out directly into their faces (you will lose customers this way).

With your product line in mind, the next thing to do is to target the customers you would like to see your ads. Facebook has a very good advertising platform where you can geo-target your customers based on their ages, genders, interests, geographical locations, education, and other things directly related to Facebook's users.

Another important thing that can make Facebook ads effective is the ad title because this is the first thing that your intended customers will see when they are on Facebook's pages. Making your ad title eye-catching and one that can really tickle the interest of your intended customers will be that ad where people can be motivated to make a click.

With your ad title already eye-catching, you have to make your ad copy also interesting and compelling.

What good will the interesting title do if your ad copy does not furnish the information that customers really need and ad texts can be abbreviated so that you can compress the information you would like to relay into the limited ad copy text.

After you have set up your ad title and contents which you created and organized so that it can give a really compelling effect, submit it to Facebook with the ad budget already set up (remember that Facebook's costs on keywords are lower than others).

You can run your ads only on a specific time frame to effectively monitor the results.

After you have made submissions of your ads to Facebook just wait for these to get displayed on Facebook's pages.

With the strict regulations imposed by Facebook, your ads may only come out after a few weeks.

FACEBOOK ADS AND HOW TO USE THEM FOR BEST RESULTS

Facebook is currently the largest social networking site in the world. The network will probably maintain its top position for years to come considering that there is no direct competition on the horizon that might knock it off the top spot.

When it comes to traffic, Facebook is now in the league of internet giants like Google, YouTube, and Wikipedia. There's no denying the fact that Facebook is among today's most influential websites.

Due to this immense popularity, Facebook has also attracted the attention of businesses, big and small. It has become a common online marketing tool. Almost every business out there is using it to promote products, services, events, and causes.

If you have a business and you are not on Facebook, you are missing out on a lot of opportunities. and exposture if your business is not on facebook. Facebook is an excellant place for businesses that want to maximize the exposure of their products and services because it has an advertising program that is specifically designed for various types of businesses. This advertising program is called Facebook Ads.

Facebook Ads work just like any self-serve online advertising program. You set up your ads, fund them with enough money, then publish them live on the social network.

Now, these ads can take different forms. If you are a Facebook user, then you are familiar with the many ways you can interact with content on the site. These interactive activities include commenting on posts, liking posts, liking pages and taking part in applications or games. These are where the Facebook ads come in, besides of course the regular ads that you see on the sidebar of your profile or account.

The ads you create will depend on what you are trying to achieve. Do you want more likes for your Facebook page? Do you want people to share your page's content? Or do you simply want to direct more traffic to your external website? These are just a few of the things you need to take into account when working with Facebook's advertising program.

HERE ARE SOME TIPS ON HOW YOU CAN USE FACEBOOK ADS FOR THE BEST RESULTS

1.   Use images well in your ads. If you look in the ads showing up in Facebook's sidebar, the ads with the best images stand out from all the rest. Learn from this and look for a visually pleasing image to use in your ad.

Of course, make sure that you have the rights or permission to use the image. Make use of the images of people as much as possible.

2.   Target your ads. When it comes to targeting ads, Facebook is unparalleled. You can target an audience by location, gender, age, relationship status, education, interests, etc.

So depending on who you want to reach, you should make use of these options when setting up your ads. This makes sure that your ads are seen by the right people.

3.   Try rotating ads. This is to test which types of ads deliver the best results. Track their performances, gather data, and then determine which ads to keep running.

4.   Write convincing and interesting ad copy. This is the text that accompanies the images in your ads

INVESTING IN FACEBOOK ADS TO GET RETURNS WITHOUT SPENDING MUCH MONEY

There are many applications available on Facebook and some of them provide us with pleasure like games. Whether you're using one of these applications for yourself or as a way of interacting with others, it can keep you busy.

In your workplace, Facebook can be helpful in refreshing your mind. It switches you from tedious, boring work to an exciting state. Remember this quote, "Too much work with less play makes Jack a dull boy."

Another thing to think about when playing around Facebook is that it's a place that attracts millions of people on a daily basis. This brings your attention that it's the best place to advertise your business and its products.

It is true that even big companies are using Facebook to promote their products.

Have you ever read a book on how some people have managed to make money on Facebook? It is true that there are some people who have managed to sell their products on Facebook. They have created a Facebook page (Facebook fan page) in order to reach potential buyers who are using Facebook (keeping in mind that there are millions of people who are currently using Facebook).

The next time you log in to Facebook, try to notice the advertisement system called Facebook ads (Advertise on Facebook). It was created because of the popularity of Facebook website among marketers. If you're unfamiliar with Facebook ads, it is basically a way to advertise a business and its products.

One of the advantages of using Facebook advertisements is that you won't worry about spending much money in order to advertise your business and its products.

Facebook advertisement option is recommended to anyone who has a short budget, unlike pay-per-click (cost per click) advertising model. Facebook ads give you the opportunity to promote your business. Remember that Facebook ads are going to be an investment for your business.

Your Facebook ad is going to persuade those people who are using Facebook to visit your business and buy your products. Facebook ads will generate traffic for your website and out of this traffic, you'll get potential buyers.

However, just like other advertisements, there is no way you'll know if Facebook ads will actually convert into profits. The effectiveness of Facebook ads depends on how persuasive your advertisements are. If your Facebook ads are persuasive, people will click them so as to buy your products. When you have known this, then it doesn't make sense to use pay-per-click advertising model since you'll spend a lot of money.

This is why it makes sense to use Facebook ads. Using Facebook ads is a great way to get started and when it works, you'll drive more targeted traffic to your online business which is also your website. Sometimes, though, the marketing ads don't turn out in a positive way.

In order to constantly improve your Facebook ads, you don't have to spend additional money. Test your advertisements for a minimum of a week while using an affordable budget. You can even test your advertisements for a couple weeks or months if you like. All this gives you an idea of what works and what doesn't. Spending a lot of money in internet marketing isn't how it works. The idea is to start small and work your way up.

HOW TO TAKE ADVANTAGE OF FACEBOOK ADS

As we all know, it's getting harder and harder to 'be seen' on Facebook since this powerhouse platform has shifted toward a pay-to-play model over the past few years.

Facebook ads and paid options still remain an effective way to target your ideal client and extend the reach of your important Facebook updates, even though many users are less than thrilled at the thought of having to pay for this option.

On a more positive note, Facebook is always striving to bring the best to its users and has recently made some changes that really give businesses the edge when it comes to reaching targeted consumers.

Are you up on the most current Facebook Ad improvements? If you aren't, you may be missing out on expanding your audience.

HERE'S WHAT'S HAPPENING WITH ONE OF THE MOST POPULAR SOCIAL MEDIA PLATFORMS

1.   Larger Ads: To some people, this may seem like a non-issue, but when you have something you really want consumers to notice, you want to go BIG. With that in mind, Facebook made the right column ads bigger and bolder. This adds more value to your advertising campaign because it gives a better impression.

Now you have more space to showcase the whole story for customers. Fewer ads on the page mean more attention to the ones that appear. Take advantage of the space and create an attention-getting ad that will lead to a higher click-through rate. Upload your creative ad on News Feed and the right column to make sure you reach your target audience.

2.   More Frequent Exposure: Remember how your mom usually had to tell you something twice before you actually heard her? Since early August advertisers have been able to use a single ad twice in the same day. This is a change from the previous once daily cap.

You can also insert ads twice a day from a page that a person is not connected to; again, an increase over the once daily cap. If a person is connected to a page, the ads from that page can still be inserted into News Feed as much as four times. That hasn't changed.

What this means for us is potential customers will see your ad twice in a day. It doesn't increase the number of ads for the consumer; only the frequency the same ad is viewed.

Facebook is constantly exploring avenues to make the Facebook experience better for consumers and business. These are just a few of the changes that have been implemented recently.

Managing Ads on the Go: As of July 2014, advertisers have a new way to manage their Facebook ads on the go with Ads Manager on mobile devices. Using the Facebook (iOS, Android, and mobile site) apps, marketers can now:

- Pause or resume campaigns

- Edit budgets and schedules

- View insights

- Respond to alerts

3. Promoted Posts: If the thought of creating and implementing a Facebook Ad still makes you cringe, there's always the super-simple Promoted Post option to fall back on. Promoted Posts are individual page posts that get additional paid reach in the News Feed among fans and

friends of fans as a result of using the page's Promote button. It's simple to use, has great analytics and allows the user to quickly select and budget using a sliding scale.

HOW MUCH DO FACEBOOK ADS COST?

One of the best options for paid advertising online is Facebook Ads. This is Facebook's advertising network, which exclusively displays your ads on the network of Facebook. The major advantage of advertising on Facebook is that you can target Facebook users with much more specificity than with any other advertising network online.

This is because people on Facebook freely give out their personal information and their interests when filling out their profiles. With this information in mind, you can target individuals on Facebook with literally an infinite number of parameters. You're not limited to interests, however. You can also search by geographic location and all kinds of personal information such as specific ages.

If you want to make an ad which only applies and will be seen by 45-year-old women who watch Glee, you can do that on and only on Facebook. This more precise targeting method yields a much healthier click through rate and a much healthier conversion of your goals.

Of course, a lot of people are wary of using paid advertising because of the obvious cost associated with it. It's not nearly as expensive as you would think, and this chapter will identify just how much you can expect to pay by explaining how much do Facebook ads cost. The number of factors determines how much does Facebook ads cost. First off, just like with

AdWords, you will get a quality score for your ad depending on a number of things.

Facebook looks at your website which you are directing your traffic towards, then it looks at how well it relates to the ad which you've just written. Sites of higher quality (more content, frequently updated, lots of backlinks, high page rank, etc.) will get you a lower CPC (cost per click).

Another thing which factors into determining how much do Facebook ads cost is the popularity of the niche which your ad targets. More popular topics which are used by other Facebook ads users are going to go for a higher cost. Less competitive niches are going to be cheaper conversely.

Your click through rate also plays a large role in determining how much your Facebook ads cost. The higher your click-through rate, the less you have to pay. The idea here is that more relevant and generally better ads lead to a higher click-through rate.

Higher clicks through rates means that you have put together a valuable ad and Facebook rewards you with a lower cost per click.

Your click through rate is easily the most dominant factor in determining how much you'll be paying.

You may be surprised that your CPC has dropped dramatically and inexplicably after your ad has been live for a while. This is because your click through rate has performed well.

HOW DO FACEBOOK ADS WORK?

Because of the popularity of Facebook and the hundreds of thousands of opportunities that it can give, many online marketers are using Facebook ads to gain wider exposure and also grow their business.

But Facebook is strict with regards to advertising, and they won't accept just any kind of ads that people will place on their site, so you have to follow their rules. Facebook is strict on everything you place the ads, the text's words, symbols, images and everything.

This is their way of making sure that you understand what you are trying to get across and also knowing what to expect out of these ads.

Facebook advertising can give additional benefits to marketers aside from wide reach, and this is through its ad cost, which is cheaper compared to other ad campaigns. If you have an ad with Facebook it means that you have to do the following things:

• You have to enter the destination URL of your ads. This is the URL link which will lead people to your website after they make a click on your Facebook ads.

• You have to provide the title of the link. This is the attractive title text that can arouse the interest of people and pay attention to your ads.

• The next thing is to provide the ad is body texts. This is the short body of your ads which indicate what you want to get across.

• Then you have to provide an image for your ads. You can choose to use the resources on Facebook in providing these images or you can provide it yourself.

- If you have an ad on Facebook, you can use your Facebook fan page as your landing page. There are so many benefits that you can get out of your Facebook ads and how these ads can work for you can be summed up with the following things:

- You can create a custom landing page on Facebook. This is what is previously mentioned where new visitors will see and this is like your home page on this social site.

- You can have images at the top of your Facebook fan page. With this opportunity, you can even have images of your products placed on these pages.

Facebook can let you have options of new visitors clicking to "like" your fan page before they can get to your other contents. This can be your way of increasing the number of your fans.

With frequent updates made to your fan page or business page, you can provide quality contents to your followers. With people getting to your page through your ads, informative contents can be gained which can possibly motivate them to make some actions, whether these are sign-ups or sales.

CHAPTER 2: WHY AND HOW TO CREATE A FAN PAGE?

Facebook is a social networking site with more than 1.86 billion monthly active users. The reason why it's so popular is because it provides a unique medium through which you can share information with friends and people who have the same interests as you do.

Facebook is easy-to-use and it's not just a great way medium to find new friends, it's also a tool that you can use to promote your business or enhance your professional profile. One of the interesting features that Facebook offers is creating a fan page.

This enables you to connect with those who are outside your Facebook friend's circle, without revealing any of your personal information. A fan page can be created for anything such as a specific event or a business promotion activity, for a public personality, a celebrity star and so on.

Creating a fan page is interesting and requires that you put in a lot of creative efforts. Here is a look at the steps involved in creating a page:

• Log into your Facebook account and find the area where you can create your Facebook fan page.

• Specify the category in which you want to be a Facebook fan. Add a name to your page.

• The "I am authorized to create this page" checkbox must be checked. Enter your name in the signature section.

• Click the 'Create Page' button to create the page. This should result in page creation of page and you can proceed to customize the page with features such as photos, personal details and much more. The steps involved in creating a Facebook page are pretty simple.

Checking out as many different fan pages as possible to add more dynamic features to your Facebook page and make it so interesting and appealing to others. Putting in new applications is one of the best ways to enhance the functionality of your Facebook account.

Once you have created a fan page, you will find people signing up for it and following you through it. If you have created a page for a business, you can post further details about that business by putting in videos, new clippings, and anything that is of interest to you.

Facebook offers a multitude of features through which you can carry out so many different activities and enjoy social networking in a larger way.

For better understanding, here are 10 simple steps: how to make a fan page on Facebook

1.   Go to this page on Facebook to create a Facebook fan page:

> Facebook.com/pages/create.php

2.   Under Official Page select either 'Local Business', 'Brand, Product or Organization' or 'Artist, band or public figure' as appropriate.

If you are creating a fan page for your business, you will likely want to select either "local business" or "brand, product or organization". Once you select, you are then asked to further categorize your fan page by selecting an option in the drop down menu. Don't worry if you cannot find your exact business category - just select the closest match.

3.   Choose a Page Name for your fan-page.

This could be the name of your business or could be the target key term that people type in to search for your product or service. You cannot change it once you have selected it - so spend a little time considering the best name for your fan page.

4.   Tick to confirm you are the official representative of the fan page.

You cannot create a page on behalf of an organization that you do not officially represent. Once you have completed the steps above, you have already got the basics of your Facebook fan page setup. The next steps are all about configuring and personalizing your Facebook Fan Page.

5.   Add a picture/image by either uploading one from your computer or taking a picture with your webcam. Use a picture/image that will best represent your brand and your business. This may be your business logo, a picture of you, a picture of your staff/ team etc.

A poor quality image will almost certainly deter potential fans; so ensure the picture you add is of adequate quality and is a good representative image for your business fan page.

6.   Provide some basic information to let your customers know more about you.

Try and add a good quality and quantity of personal information to clearly communicate what you and your business are about, what makes you different, your mission. People buy from people - so try and be friendly and personable.

Include a link to your website if you have one.

7.   Click the blue Photos tab, and create a Photo Album.

This is a really effective way to add a personal touch to your Facebook fan page. As mentioned above, people buy from people; so some natural photo's of you, you at work, your premises, your staff/team, your family etc; can make a real difference to the impact of your fan page.

8.   Click the blue Discussions tab and Start a New Topic of discussion.

Choose a really catchy and highly targeted discussion related to your business. Discussions are a great way to increase engagement with your fans/visitors and get them involved. You do not just have to start one discussion - start 3-5 interesting and topical discussions if you wish to add more content to your page at the outset.

9.   Just below your main picture/image (top left), there is a link "Edit Page".

Under "Settings" > Click "Edit".

a.   Country Restrictions. If you wish to target specific countries, enter them here. People from other countries will not be able to access your fan page.

b.   Age Restrictions. You may wish to limit access to people over the age of 18, or 21. Select as appropriate.

c.   Published. You may wish to keep your page unpublished until it is fully set up and ready to promote.

d.   Under Wall > click "edit".

We recommend you ensure the default view of the wall is "all posts" - and leave all other settings under "wall" as they are by default.

10.   Launch.

Update the status on your wall. This will be your first post on your new fan page wall, so make it a good one. Start as you mean to go on. Click "suggest to friends" - which is located under the profile image on your new fan page. You can choose to send a message to ALL the friends in your main Facebook account, or to a selection of your friends.

When it comes to your Facebook page, the first thing you want to think about is if you can grow a quality fan base there, if people are engaging with you. Engagement is really specific. If you can get people to click like on your post, comment, share, or click a link that's engagement. That's when Facebook says okay people are engaging with your Facebook page, let's push you out into the news feed more often so people see your post.

CHAPTER 3: INSTALL FACEBOOK PIXELS

In this chapter, we'll explain how to create a Facebook pixel, add its base code to your website, add its event code to your website and define conversions.

To do:

• Create a Facebook pixel

• Add the Facebook pixel base code to all your website's pages

• Add the event code to some of your website's pages

• Confirm your pixel is implemented correctly

Creating a Facebook pixel

To create your Facebook pixel:

Go to your Facebook Pixel tab in Ads Manager.

Click Create a Pixel.

Facebook pixel code

The Facebook pixel code is made up of two main elements:

Pixel base code

Event code

The pixel base code tracks activity on your website, providing a baseline for measuring specific events. The base code should be installed on every page of your website.

To install the pixel base code:

Go to the Pixel page in Ads Manger

Click Actions > View Code

Copy the base code and paste it between the <head> tags on each web page, or in your website template to install it on your entire website

Events are actions that happen on your website, either as a result of Facebook ads (paid) or organic reach (unpaid). The event code lets you track those actions and leverage them in advertising.

There are two types of events you can send:

Standard events. 9 events we're able to track and optimize your ads for without any additional actions. See below for an example of what your website code will look like with standard events installed.

Enter a name for your pixel. You can have only one pixel per ad account, so choose a name that represents your business.

Note: You can change the name of the pixel later from the Facebook Pixel tab.

Check the box to accept the terms.

Click Create Pixel.

The new Facebook pixel makes conversion tracking, optimization and remarketing easier than ever. Use the new pixel with standard events and you'll be able to access all features below.

Conversion tracking. See how successful your ad is by seeing what happened as a direct result of your ad.

Optimization. Automatically bid for conversions after you set up your pixel.

Retargeting. Remarket to everyone who visits your site, or just to people who visit specific pages or take specific actions.

Put your pixel to work

When you add standard events, your conversions are tracked across mobile phones, tablets and desktop computers.

When you optimize your bids for website conversions, your ads will only show to people who are most likely to convert.

You can also remake or reach people on Facebook who already visited your website. For example, people who visited your checkout page, but not your order confirmation page.

You can also use the Facebook pixel to find new customers who are similar to your website visitors by creating a lookalike audience. Create a lookalike audience once your pixel takes a minimum of 100 conversions.

BENEFITS OF THE FACEBOOK PIXEL

1.   Ad optimization: When you use the Facebook pixel in combination with the bidding option Optimize for Website Conversions, Facebook will automatically show your ads to people who are most likely to convert.

2.   Measurement: You can measure the number of conversions your ads generate to calculate your return on ad spend. That way you'll see how much you're spending for each conversion and can fine-tune your ads accordingly.

SET UP CONVERSION TRACKING

See how your ads perform by using standard events or Custom Conversions. Both make it easy to measure the performance of your Facebook ads, and to reach specific sets of people who have visited certain pages of your website.

Standard events represent the types of actions people take on your website, for example where people make purchases. You can set this up by adding a snippet of code to your Facebook Pixel.

Custom Conversions also lets you track conversions and set up audiences for remarketing by entering the URL you want to see directly into Ads Manager. If you don't want to add text to your pixel code, learn how to set up a custom conversion.

MEASURE THE RESULTS OF YOUR FACEBOOK ADS

Conversion measurement lets you track actions people take after viewing your Facebook Ads across multiple devices, including mobile phones, tablets, and desktop computers.

By creating a Facebook pixel and adding it to the pages of your website where conversions happen, like the checkout page, you'll see who converts as a result of your Facebook Ads.

The pixel will continue to monitor the actions people take after clicking on your ad. You can see which device they saw the ad on and which device they ultimately converted on.

ADD THE FACEBOOK PIXEL TO YOUR WEBSITE

Install Pixel:

To add the pixel to your website, take the code and place it between <head></head> in the code of the webpage that you want to track conversions on.

This pixel can track conversions such as checkouts, registrations, leads, key page views or customers adding items to a cart. Be sure to add the pixel to the page on your site where conversions take place.

You can also assign a value to the conversion event.

Verify Pixel:

Once you've created your pixel, you can see its status. Until you've had a conversion, the status will show as unverified. Your pixel must be installed properly and record a conversion event to become verified so that you can begin using it.

Use the pixel for ad optimization

Once you've placed the tracking code on your website, it's time to start creating ads.

Create a new ad in the ads create a tool or in the Power Editor in Chrome

Select Increase conversions on your website

From the drop-down box, select the name of the conversion pixel you would like to use in your ad, or create a new pixel

Set up the rest of your ad targeting. In the final Bidding and Pricing section, choose Website Conversions to show your ads automatically to people more likely to convert.

Note: Facebook tracks conversions for ads that happen within 1 day, 7 days and 28 days after a person clicks on an ad, and 1 day, 7 days and 28 days after viewing an ad

If you have already created a thank you page in LeadPages for example, go into your LeadPagesTM account and Edit your Thank You Page. Click the LeadPage Options, and Tracking Codes. Paste the code into the Head[Tag Tracking Code box on that Thank You Page. Now, whenever someone visits that page, the Conversion Pixel alerts Facebook of their activity (repeat this process for your Sales Conversion Pixel).

MEASURE CONVERSIONS

After creating the ad, you'll see relevant columns from the Ads view in Ads Manager to monitor your conversions, including Results (conversions you've received) and Cost (cost per conversion). These columns link directly back to the ad within the ad set and campaign you created under the Website Conversions objective, so you can properly track the impact of your campaign. Examples of conversions you're tracking from your Facebook Ads includes checkouts, sign-ups, and leads.

CHAPTER 4: HOW TO ADVERTISE ON FACEBOOK

Facebook is probably the largest social media sites out there in the online world. There are millions of active users on that site sharing their information and experiences.

People take advantage of this huge number to advertise their services and products. Just imagine having a promotional campaign to millions of users daily. That's a massive benefit to all the internet marketers because they don't have to spend much time promoting through other methods.

There are generally two ways that you can advertise on Facebook.

1.   The Freeway

2.   The Paid way

1.   THE FREEWAY

A free way of promoting through Facebook is pretty easy. Facebook allows users to set up a page to promote their businesses. A Facebook page is basically a one-page site with information and description of what you are trying to sell or services that you offer. A page can be "Shared" to other users or "Liked".

Over time, your page will be visible to a lot of people and all you have to do is update what is going on with your business on that page. Updating your page regularly will add more content and information about what are you trying to sell thus this is a great way to "pre-sell" your prospects and you will have a higher conversion rate from prospects to buyers.

Other than that, you can simply create a profile page on Facebook and build a great relationship with other users on the site. By doing this, you can find out what is needed by your prospects and improve your products and services.

Also, people are more likely to buy from someone that they trust and have a great relationship with.

2.   THE PAID WAY

Facebook offers advertisers to promote their products or services through the pay-per-click advertising system that they have on the site. Basically, you create an ad on Facebook and direct the ad to what you are offering. Then, you specify what category of audience you would like to have your ad visible to. The options that are available include:

- Location

- Age

- "Interests" (they have the option to include their interests in their profile)

Provided that you have researched your niche thoroughly, you will have an easy time separating who are going to see your ad and who won't. For example, if you are selling a book in the wedding niche, you can specify your ad to be visible to newlyweds or engaged couples instead of blasting your ad to 15-year-old users. Using Facebook as a promoting tool can be a real advantage to you, but you have to know the right way of doing this.

HOW TO ADVERTISE ON FACEBOOK LIKE A PRO

When you think about advertising on Facebook, it is good to plan some basic key steps that will make your campaign to meet the desired goals that classic post boosting will not be able to achieve.

The first step is to precisely define the target group you want to reach with your campaign and you can get help from Facebook tools for creating adverts that offer the possibility of elaborating target groups by age, gender, interests, locations and behavior.

After that, it is necessary to provide an adequate budget so the advertisement can reach the required number of people. However, the most important part is to determine the goal of your advertisement campaigns. Your goals must be simple and the results of the campaign by which to evaluate the effectiveness of advertisement are easily measurable.

In order to facilitate campaign management for advertisers, Facebook has determined 14 different goals in its tools for creating adverts, Power Editor that you can achieve with your adverts. Below we explain in more detail each of the available options.

1.   Click for website

This type of advertisement is used for people who have an online destination page where there are facilities for which you want to reach the target groups. One of the reasons for the activation of this advert can be branded, creating and raising awareness of your product or service to the desired audience.

2.   Page post engagements

Page Post Engagements are also commonly used in the construction of the image of the brand, but also to raise engagement on the fan pages. The goal of this advert is to show fan pages to specific user groups to enable them to perform their particular activity.

3.   Page likes

Page Likes are used to build a Facebook community or increase the number of fans. They are used in addition to building the brands that specific users will become fans of the page.

4.   Event responses

Event Responses are ideal for pages on Facebook that regularly create Facebook events and the advertisement makes it possible to see the event and respond to it by all interested users who are or are not members of your community and all those outside your circle of friends on Facebook.

5.   Video views

Facebook video is becoming an increasingly important segment in the digital marketing. It can quickly send a message to the target group who are interested in your products and services. Video Views advertisement allows the video to display to as many people as possible.

6.   Offer claims

If you often create short-term actions and offers for your products, this advert is for you. They can precisely define the quantity that you want to offer while users are able to download a special code by which to accomplish special price for a particular product.

7.   Lead generations

If you are using a newsletter or some other form of communication for which users needs to fill a form with their personal data, I recommended this type of advert for you. To all users who access Facebook via mobile devices these ads will simply help them to fill in the form with the needed data.

8.   Local awareness

If you want your Facebook advert to be shown to people at a location near your business, the first choice should be the Local Awareness advert so that all the users that are closer to the location will know about your new little neighborhood store.

9.   Product catalog sales

For all the owners of web shops with a wide range of products, the ideal choice for the Facebook advert is the Product Catalog Sales which displays all the products from the webshop depending on the user and their interests.

10.   Website conversions

Website Conversions are used when you want the user to perform some specific actions such as registering for your newsletter, fill in the contact form or purchase your product.

The advertisement accurately tracks how many actions have been accomplished and you have a detailed review of the budget spent for each of them.

11.   Mobile App installations

If your company has a mobile application through this Mobile App Installation advert it is possible to find new users to download the application to their smartphone.

12.   Mobile App engagements

Mobile App Engagement can increase the activity of the existing user applications. The application with information about flight connections and the ability to purchase air tickets can advertise special flight tickets to certain users.

13.   Desktop App installations

Similar to the mobile application, Desktop App Installation is just when people download desktop applications.

14.   Desktop App engagements

Desktop App Engagement can increase the activity of existing users of your desktop applications. Finally, it is important to know that a single advert can have only one of the goals listed above. Before every campaign, you should always make it clear what you want to achieve and engage experts in setting up your advertisement.

Which Kind of Campaign?

There's cost per click, there's cost per conversion(lead or sale), and there's CPM, or cost per thousand impressions.

The question is, which of those do you feel are the key metrics that you want people to be paying attention to?

The answer depends on your goals. So, if you are looking to drive website conversion, you should be going with cost per conversion. If you're looking for general traffic based on your cost per thousand, then your cost per click will be your biggest metric. Alternatively, if you're looking for an actual shopping cart purchase on your site, cost per customer or cost per checkout is going to be your biggest metric to keep an eye on.

Conversions

There are two types of conversions. There are leads and there are sales.

If you're using LeadPages, which I personally recommend, then the cost per lead is going to be the biggest metric for you.

The metric that you should rely on from Facebook's side of things is the cost per lead or cost to acquire an email address.

Next, we will look at some things that people will be thinking about from the start,which help drive the cost per lead down.

I definitely believe that keeping an eye on metrics on a daily basis or even a couple of times a day helps. The faster you can turn something off that's not working, the more you cut that excess spending that ultimately makes your cost per lead go up.

Targeting is another big point to keep in mind. If you find someone who is genuinely interested in what you have to offer from the start, then that conversion rate is going to be a lot better on your landing page, which ultimately ends up resulting in a lower cost per lead.

So, as you're looking at the cost per lead as a metric, you need to know a few things about Facebook's environment. This knowledge will help you understand what to put on your own websites, LeadPages, and your Facebook pages in order to make sure that that cost per lead number is actually accurately reported.

Facebook allows you to create as many conversion pixels as you would like. Then, you place that snippet of code on the thank you page behind your LeadPage. That way, Facebook knows somebody got to that page, which means the client has given you their email address, and then Facebookcountsit as a lead or a conversion, a registration, or whatever you're calling it inside of Facebook.

I think anytime you have a valuable asset that somebody would like to download, whether it's a webinar, white paper, PDF, or something that gives value to someone, you can run an ad campaign around it. If you're posting especially frequently on a blog, I think you should be posting that on Facebook as well and then running paid placements for those Facebook posts. If you produce valuable content, it's very easy to promote that content using Facebook advertising and all of its features. So, at my company, we've seen good results andpositive returns on advertising, just by promoting our own content that we produce.

So, free reports, free downloads, and webinar registrations are good places for people to go to and enter their email addresses in exchange for content.Then, they're on your email list and you can market to them afterwards.

Most definitely, anytime that you have an e-commerce shopping cart, sending retargeting traffic or at least testing the process of sending retargeting traffic right to the shopping cart is a good approach.

You or your website operators may go in and set up some audiences for people who have been to your pricing page. If visitors have had enough interest to get all the way to your pricing page, then you can retarget them and send them directly to the shopping cart page or to the pricing page where they can purchase.

If someone shows enough intent, however, you define it from a website traffic perspective, you can send them right to your pricing page. However, most models suggest that you go for lead opt-in first and get them warm through some sort of nurturing sequence. Then, perhaps down the road, send them to a thank you page.

I think the more directly targeted your ads are and the more you can speak to your targeted audience, the better off you are from a click rate, from a conversion rate, and from basically every metric that you want to improve. The more targeted you can get with your ads, the better.

Anytime you can get traffic to your site and start collecting data on your site or your landing page, you stand to benefit from that information.

It is commonly believed that sending traffic within Facebook will reduce your costs.

You may see a lower cost per click and you may see a lower cost per thousand sending them to a Facebook page, but in my experience, I've seen a lot lower conversion rate from this tactic and it's still been cost-effective to send traffic to our own site.

CHAPTER 5: FIVE DIFFERENT AUDIENCES YOU CAN REACH

It's essential that you take advantage of the existing relationship that you have with your current and growing audiences with Facebook's Custom Audience options.

Facebook allows you to run ads for five different types of audiences. Each one is important for different reasons. The first three audiences are people who have an existing relationship with you, either on or off Facebook.

First, is your Facebook Fans (and their friends). If you've been building up a community on Facebook, then this is a great group to start with. You don't have to do anything else to prepare that audience for marketing.

Second, Facebook lets you advertise directly to your database of customers or subscribers that you've gathered off Facebook. This group is frequently overlooked by new Facebook advertisers, but they are a great group to target because they come with a lower cost-per-click on average. Additionally, like your Facebook fans, members of this audience are already familiar with you.

Third, you can target people who have visited particular pages on your website, thanks to Facebook Pixel.

Let's get started creating your audiences.

In your Ads Manager, choose Audiences from the menu, then click the green Create Audience button in the top right corner.

We're going to start by advertising to your existing customers, subscribers, and connections, so click on Custom Audience.

Click Customer List to upload a list of subscribers, buyers, or connections that you have gathered over the life of your business. To ensure you have a high-quality list, I recommend you never purchase a leads list and use it for this purpose.

Make sure that whatever list you use at least includes your audience members' email addresses. You can also add people by their phone numbers or other information.

In order to get your customer data, you'll need to download a file from online and offline databases.

Your email service provider will likewise have a subscriber export for you in the form of a .CSV file.

You can advertise directly to your connections on Google, Google Plus, and LinkedIn. Very few people take advantage of this hidden feature that these social networks offer, but it may prove highly beneficial to you.

To get your Google and Google Plus contacts, go to myaccount.google.com and login if you are not already logged in. In Account Settings, look for the Account Tools area, and then Download Data. Click Select None, and then check Contacts and Google+ Circles. Click the little drop-down arrow to change the data from a vCard to a .CSV file for both types of data.

At the bottom of the page, click Next. Choose the .zip file format for your archive, and click Create Archive. Download the file when it's ready, and look for the All Contacts .CSV file in your Contacts folder, as well as the various .CSV files of the Circles you've created inside the Google+ Circles folder. Review the information in the spreadsheet and clean it up if necessary.

To get your LinkedIn Connections list, log in to your LinkedIn account, and click Connections in the primary menu.

On the far right of the next page, click the small gear icon to get to your Connections settings. Click Export LinkedIn Connections in the Advanced Settings area on the right side of the settings.

Then choose Export to Microsoft Outlook (.CSV) from the dropdown menu and save the file to your computer.

Return to your Facebook Custom Audience creation screen and choose Upload File.

The next audience to create is your Retargeting Audience. Even if you've got very little traffic coming to your site now, setting up Retargeting will save you a lot of money and make you a lot of money over time. Plus, even if you aren't ready to start running paid ads on Facebook, you should still create a Retargeting Audience today because it will allow Facebook to start collecting valuable data for you.

From the Audience screen, choose Create Audience, then Custom Audience.This time, select Website Traffic.

You can create a few different retargeting audiences, but the most important step right now is to create a general retargeting audience of everybody who visits your site.

Make sure "Anyone who visits your website" is selected in the drop-down menu, and then enter the primary website address. Then, name your audience for easy reporting. You will likely create several audiences, so make sure you name your audience in such a way that makes perfect sense to you.

Just retargeting, in general, is delivering an ad to somebody who has been to at least any one page on your site.

I recommend choosing everywhere on your site so you can retarget all of that traffic. The algorithm then attaches cookies to each visitor. Then, you can follow those people and deliver them an ad for your business or your service when they come back to Facebook.

At this point, you might be asking: is there a reason why you would use a different retargeting pixel on different parts of your website depending on what behavior someone has exhibited on your site?

In other platforms, it actually works like that. However, the glory of Facebook lies in the fact that they allow you to put one retargeting pixel on your whole site.Then, inside of the Facebook ads platform, you can start to segment your traffic based on what page they went to and whether they got to the thank you page. So, Facebook's advertising platform actually works a lot easier than do other retargeting platforms because it's just one pixel across your whole site. That would be important for somebody to use because once somebody has bought your product, you want to save a little money and not keep sending them ads for the thing that they've already bought.

So, you would create two different audiences, one for someone who has been to your site and one for someone who has been to your site and got to the thank you page. Then, you can exclude that second audience from your ads. You've already got their email addresses. They've already purchased a product from you now, so it would be of no use to spend money on them anymore.

The fourth audience is critical for scaling your advertising campaigns. Once you have a good custom audience in place, Facebook allows you to create a Lookalike Audience, which targets hundreds of thousands or millions of users that Facebook has determined look like your custom audience.

Lookalike Audiences are exactly what they sound like: audiences of Facebook users who "look like" the custom audiences that you created.

We'll start by selecting the Create Audience, Lookalike Audience option from the Facebook ads Audience dashboard. Choose the source of your Lookalike Audience by choosing one of the custom audiences you created.

Next, choose the size of your Lookalike Audience. I recommend you keep this number on the smaller side for two reasons. First, the smaller the group, the better match Facebook makes the audience. Second, the narrower your group, the less wasted spending you'll have with your campaigns.

Keep your Target Groups narrow. Even though Facebook can give you huge audiences, you'll be better served by targeting groups of 50,000 to 100,000 for effective campaigns.

Lookalike audiences are great, especially when it comes to expansion and when you think you've run out of ideas for audiences to target. Facebook has got an algorithm and I don't know if anyone knows exactly how it works. But, they take all the data from your retargeting pixel. Facebook will gather data from somebody who's been to your site. Then, they mirror it with the whole population that uses Facebook and, based on attributes, they come up with a group that looks like people who have been to your site. You can even get more finite and come up with a lookalike audience that looks like your customers.

They may have never converted on your site, but, based on Facebook's algorithm, if Facebook says that this audience looks like your customers, then they must act like your customers online.According to successful online marketers, Lookalikes are a good group to target.

You make sure Facebook knows which pages on your site are checkout pages so that Facebook will inform you of which people have become customers. Then, Facebook figures out an audience that looks like that based on those people's behavior on Facebook, their interest levels, and their online activity.

The best thing that Facebook has to offer from the advertising side of things is just the ability to get your ad in front of eyeballs that, at least from an algorithm standpoint, should be looking at your ad.

The fifth audience allows you to target users of Facebook based on a large number of factors, including location, gender, age, behaviors, interests, and more demographics. This is an important group to target, but I encourage you to build this type of audience last because of how much more profitable the other four audiences tend to be.

You can get as broad as you want or as finite as you want but I always recommend as finite as possible right away. Use the targeting capabilities, even if it's just a small audience. Find something that works and then start to expand from there. Rather than using the shotgun approach of "Hey we're going to throw ads out to everyone," which I did unsuccessfully at the start of my online business endeavors, you should really try to target down to a small audience. Start there, find something that works, and then expand on that.

CHAPTER 6: LANDING PAGES AND FACEBOOK ADS

With LeadPagesTM templates, you'll be able to create amazing pages in less than 30 minutes or even faster as you repeat the process. There will be no need to go back and forth with a web designer who might take 2 weeks to finish your page. Plus, you'll be able to make any changes you want without having to get back on their schedule.

I recommend using your landing page as a lead collector instead of a sale generator. Unless you're retargeting interested people who are familiar with your brand using a custom audience campaign, your best bet is to advertise to an opt-in page instead of a sales page.

Your landing page should have a high Call to Action button above the fold, and be clickable towards a two-step opt-in form. Do not just have an opt-in form on the page itself.

Ideally, you should create a different landing page for each Target Audience that you are marketing to. The more your landing page matches the expectation set from your Ad and your Target Audience, the more likely you are to convert that click into a lead.

You should also provide something of value that's simple to understand and realize the benefit from. Webinars are hot right now, and it's no surprise to us that webinar registration pages are the highest converting landing pages in the LeadPagesTM system. People respond well to webinars because there is a built-in sense of urgency, and they typically go more in-depth to solve a problem than an average e-book does.

You may also want to give away a free resource guide, e-book, mind map, or audio that delivers instant gratification to your new visitor.

Here are a few more tips about high converting landing pages:

. Landing page text and imagery should match the promise of your Facebook Ad.

. Landing pages should comply with Facebook's ever-changing terms of service.

. Landing pages should be easy for you to quickly adjust, split test, and duplicate, based on your individual campaigns.

Ideally, you'll advertise directly from Facebook to your Opt-In pages. Then, in your email follow-up, drive your interested subscribers to the Sales page. Also, once you have traffic to your Sales page, you can use that Custom Audience pixel to run Retargeting Ads to the people who have seen your offer but are yet to buy.

Choose any LeadPageTM template you want to use, and customize the text, images, and color styles. The main difference between a Sales page and an Opt-In page is the function of the Call to Action button. Simply click the gear icon for your button and change the purpose of the button from Show Opt-in Form to Go To URL. Use the payment link you get from your shopping cart or merchant account to connect your LeadPageTM to your checkout process.

Remember, you'll also want to add your Custom Audience pixel to all of your LeadPagesTM you create. Go to LeadPagesTM options, and then

Tracking Codes. Paste your pixel in this head tag box. Remember, this is not the same as the Conversion Pixel. You'll use that on the Thank You page in a moment.

To publish my page, I can choose to use the LeadPages.net server, publish to WordPress on my own site, show it as a tab on my Facebook page, or host it on my own server outside of WordPress. I'll use the WordPress plug-in to add it to my own domain in just a couple of clicks.

I'll click the LeadPagesTM tab in WordPress, then Add New. I'll choose the page from the drop-down menu, and create the slug I want on my domain. I'll hit Publish, and I'm all set with my page.

You can also publish your pages to Facebook, and you'll usually see a lower cost per click when you do so. But we find that the conversions for pages published to Facebook don't typically justify that route because the average Facebook user can get easily distracted by more notifications and other ads while they're looking at your offer. So, we recommend sending your Facebook ad traffic off Facebook for maximum conversions. It also helps your retargeting efforts later if the visitors go to a site that you control.

If you do want to publish to Facebook, it's easy to do in just a few clicks. Click Publish to Facebook, select the Page you want it on, and you're done.

CHAPTER 7: SIDE-SCROLLING CAROUSEL ADS

Facebook recently added a feature known as Carousel Ads. When users come across a Carousel Ad, they have the option to scroll from side-to-side in order to view up to ten different pieces of content that the advertiser has placed in one "carousel."

Carousel Ads are great choices for advertisers who believe that they will benefit from having their audiences view many different photos, videos, links, headlines, or calls to actions in one interaction.

In order for a Facebook user to view the entirety of a side-scrolling Carousel Ad, they must manually scroll or swipe through that advertisement. These advertisements tend to be a bit more interactive than other formats.

Most commonly, advertisers use this format when they need to show off a variety of offerings in order to have a successful advertising campaign. For example, many online retailers make use of the Carousel format in order to show off some of the many products that they sell. News organizations often place several headlines in one side-scrolling Carousel Ad. Alternatively, if you are selling a product that has many specific details, you can use a Carousel Ad to showcase several photographs of the same item, with each image portraying a different important detail of your offering. Some creative advertisers tell a story using this format.

To create your own Carousel Ad, log on to your Facebook Page. Then, find the button near the uppermost right corner of the screen that says Promote; click it. Select the option that reads Promote Your Website. Facebook will then prompt you to upload content for your Carousel. Follow their prompts and, when you are finished adding content to your Ad, click the link that says Promote. Your Ad Manager will provide you with valuable feedback pertaining to your Carousel Ads' performances.

Facebook is still working on the video portion of Carousel Ads. The ability to include more than one video in the same Carousel Ad is only available to a very limited number of advertisers at the time of the writing of this book. Facebook intends to make that feature available to all advertisers in the future, however. Additionally, if you do have the ability to include multiple videos in the same Carousel Ad, you will not be able to see the view counts for each individual video. Rather, Facebook will only provide you with the total combined number of views from all of the videos in your Ad together.

CHAPTER 8: FACEBOOK ADS AND COPYWRITING

Writing effective ad copy for your Facebook ads is more important than most advertisers think.

First, your ad needs to pass the Facebook review process, which monitors ad content to conform to their ever-evolving guidelines. And, once it's approved, you want to be certain it's going to be effective in reaching your desired goal.

Here are 3 things you can do to ensure success with your ad copy:

1.   Make sure your message is clear and concise

When you write your Facebook ad, make sure that your message answers at least one of these questions (more is better):

a.   What is the ad about?

b.   Who is the ad intended to reach?

c.   What does the ad want the reader to do?

Say, for example, that your ad is aiming to bring more awareness to your brand. By relating your brand's image to the readers and how it can help them, you are addressing two of the above questions in one shot, because you acknowledge something about the reader's needs while explaining something about your brand.

2.   Include a strong call to action and a powerful headline

When you create your Facebook ad, you'll be short-changing your results if you don't include a strong call to action. A call to action might include simple phrases like "click here," "buy now," or "discover more."

Your call to action will typically need to be short and sweet, particularly if you are running a right side ad on Facebook. Newsfeed ads will actually give you the option to include a call to action button in your ad.

About the headline, It has to be a question that the answer that you want them to come up with in their head is a yes. You wouldn't want to ask them a question that their initial answer is going to be no.

3.   Don't publish a copy without another set of eyes

This is especially important if you are new to writing Facebook ad copy, but would certainly be a good idea for anyone. Not only will an editor (formal or informal) ensure that your ad runs without any grammar or spelling errors, but they'll also help you be certain that your ad copy makes sense.

Another set of eyes on your ad will help you avoid publishing ads that will inherently fail. Creating successful ad copy doesn't come naturally to everyone. So take the time to do some research, taking note of other ads that you want to emulate as you are creating your own ads.

And, if you are ever in doubt, it might be worth the investment to engage a professional firm or consultant to help you get your first few campaigns up and running.

Finally, you can always use Facebook's own detailed help section to learn the do's, don't, and best practices of Facebook advertising.

CHAPTER 9: HOW TO REDUCE COSTS ON FACEBOOK

The one truth about doing business today is no business can survive and grow without advertising. Companies spend huge sums of money on advertising.

For large and well-established businesses, the cost of advertising is easily born, but this is not the case for small and medium size businesses. Therefore, these businesses are constantly looking for opportunities to reduce the cost of their advertising.

The huge number of people who use Facebook makes it an ideal platform for businesses to reach out to potential clients. Many businesses can attest to the fact that using Facebook can lead to significant growth in income as a result of increased visibility.

But the question most business owners ask is whether advertising on Facebook is free or not. The answer to this question depends on the kind of advertising you are looking for.

The Facebook platform offers a huge opportunity for all businesses around the world to advertise their products for free. However, success depends on the creativity of the individual businessperson. It is just a matter of taking advantage of the various tools and options provided by Facebook: individual accounts, pages, forums, and groups can all be used for free to publicize a business.

You can use your personal page to introduce your products and services to your friends. Depending on how you present the information, your friends' friends may see the product or service posted on their wall. And, if your friends have bigger networks, then you end up reaching a larger market than you expect.

Another way of advertising for free on Facebook is by joining discussion groups and forums related to your line of business. You don't join and immediately start promoting a product or a business.

You first take the time to acquaint yourself with the members and learn the rules of the group. You then establish yourself as a credible member by making meaningful contributions in the form of comments and posts. It is only after this that you can introduce your own products and services.

You can also create a free page for your products or business, and link this page to your website so that people who visit your page are linked directly to your website.

On the other hand, placing a Facebook "Like" button on your website gives visitors the opportunity to promote your business for you, free of charge.

Apart from these free opportunities, there is what is referred to as Facebook ads proper. This is a system put in place by the owners of Facebook to generate income for the site.

These ads are not free and work like Google AdWords. You set your own cost and Facebook will give you a package to suit your budget. It has been argued that Facebook ads are not as rewarding as making use of the platform itself. Facebook ads should be used as a complement to the free opportunities available on the platform.

Facebook has all it takes for businesses to advertise for free. Businesses should learn to take advantage of these opportunities.

HOW TO REDUCE YOUR FACEBOOK ADVERTISING COST

If you have an Internet business it is more likely that you will invest in advertising on the net to ensure that you will attain the success for your business.

Facebook advertising is a good way to attain this business success, considering its capabilities to cover a wide reach, with its hundreds of millions of active users.

So if you advertise on Facebook, not only will it cost less but also have more tendencies to send people directly to your landing page or fan page than sending them directly to your website. And through this way, it will be more likely to retain your audience and gain their trust later, which can probably result in sales in the future.

But first, you have to understand the difference between advertising in Facebook with its cost per click (CPC) scheme and cost per thousand impressions (CPM) compared to those ads with the other networks.

Therefore, Facebook advertisements operate on a platform that is based upon various demographics of users of which you are planning to target, like if you opt to target specific age levels, educational levels, genders, or other user's specifics.

As previously mentioned, advertising on this social site is so cheap compared to the other ad programs on other networks and you will notice this if you try it the first time.

And therefore considering its unique way of targeting users, you will not experience it with anything else online.

However, by advertising on Facebook your first toy with cost per click as definitely it is much cheaper than the cost per thousand impressions. You will notice that this is also true with ad programs with the other networks.

By starting off with opting for pay per click, Facebook will give you a suggested bid range with a certain amount. Do not bid on the lowest amount in the suggested bid range and run your ads. You will notice that your Facebook ads will have tendencies to get approved provided you follow its guidelines thoroughly.

But once your ads are already running do not stop there, but continue monitoring your click through and if you become aware that you are not getting enough then it is necessary that you bid more.

If you want your ads to maintain the lesser cost do not wait for Facebook to increase your suggested bid range, which can happen if you are not getting a considerable conversion and Facebook will stop running your ads.

Once this happens your suggested bid range will increase, so before this happens you have to increase your bid slightly higher than your first and run your ads again.

HOW TO REDUCE YOUR CPC ON FACEBOOK ADS

CPC experts have concluded that CPCs are lower if the linked site to the ad is connected to an internal page. This is because there are links outside that entail further costs to maintain.

The specific underlying reasons are quite complicated and technical in their inherent characteristics, that's' why more site owners are turning to CPC consultants to ramp up their earnings. The affective factors may include the demographic of the target market, the timing of the ad's release, Facebook audience specific factors, and the like.

Second, it is widely known that when you have a higher CTR, your CPC will lower (similar to Google). If linking to an internal fan page, your ad you should always give a reason for someone to "Like" your fan page. Through split testing, we have found that the CTR is incredibly high when we use a simple ad such "Click like if you like XYZ".

An example, could be if you are creating a fan page for basketball tricks, you could simply target Facebook users that have basketball as an interest and then you could create an ad stating "Click Like if you like basketball" or "Click Like if you want to play like Lebron James".

That is just one example and you can alter it to your liking. Never underestimate the power of huge crowds. The best way to attract a crowd of internet traffic (translatable to sales) is to have a huge number of members already subscribed to your advertised site.

This is the power of numbers and having followers follow the pack. All fan pages start at 0 so try your best to get your internal network to like your page. Another way to drop your Facebook ad CPC is by targeting your market. In the ad options, there is a way to specify the gender, age, demographic and interest of your target market. When specifying the interest of your market, it is very important that you specify only one or two interests for your ad.

The reason for this is that since it is more targeted it will lower your CPC. You will need to create multiple ads which will have different targeted interests, but the same ad image and copy. This will also help you determine which ads are most effective and eliminate the higher CPC ads.

Finally, probably the most important feature of your ad on Facebook is your ad image. This ad image should not be complimentary colors to Facebook (blue and white) and should be an image that really stands out from the rest.

You could use the most beautifully photographed image, but if someone doesn't notice it in their peripheral vision, you are out of luck. We once ran an ad that was a bottle of milk with the words "Raw" over top. Quite possibly, it was the ugliest ad on Facebook, but it had a great response and provided a great conversion rate. Remember, the more clicks you have, the lower your CPC will be.

It is vital to split test your ads and see what is the most effective ad for you. If you are driving traffic to an internal Facebook Fan Page, you will want to monitor how many likes you are receiving vs. clicks. Through our split testing, we have managed to have a good rate of 80% conversion.

A click through rate below 0.1% usually means you need to adjust the ad. Facebook ads can be an excellent resource to generate more business if used properly. The lowest CPC we have tested has been 0.01. There are advertisers out there that have been below 1 cent clicks.

CHAPTER 10: SPLIT TEST AND MULTIPLE ADS IN FEW SECONDS

WHAT IS SPLIT TESTING?

Split testing is nothing more than testing different variations within your PPC campaign to see which variation gives you the best results and in the end the best bang for your buck.

It is advised to always split test any time you begin to pay per click marketing, never start a campaign with a bunch of keywords and let it run as it is. To those of you who have not heard of split testing, well, so that you now know, split testing is an invaluable part of running a successful online marketing and advertising campaign.

In another word; to define the process further, split testing or sometimes called A/B testing is changing a component of the ad while maintaining all the other variables as they originally were and doing this one item at a time to determine which ad is performing better and which one is not.

Now there is a specific way on how to perform split testing and at the same time analyze the numbers so let us try to see what they are. The major variables in your ad are the targeting (pertains to the process by which the ad marks a customer), the copy, the images or pictures, and the title.

Now in order for split testing to be accurate, or at least very near it, the ads once altered should be run under the very same conditions as before - same time, same day, same bid, same length of time, and all the other conditions that were present during the initial running, and if these conditions are not met, then the results cannot be deemed as conclusive since the circumstances of the two testing events were not the same and there may be variables that contribute to the former result that is not present on the second one and vice versa.

Look closely at the reports and focus on what specific ad did well, and this process is a bit tricky because I have seen sites with multiple visitors yet the conversions are minimal, so focus on conversions and gauge the ad's success on that.

Be creative by making new ads, do not try to fix an ad if it does not perform great, discard it and change it and you may even use the Facebook "Create a Similar Ad" tab to assist you and you get to keep your settings as well.

In Facebook ads, the primary things to monitor closely are clicked, the click-through rates or CTR, actions, action rates, and the CPC and all these variables differ from each other especially you are running a special type of ad campaign. However, always keep in mind that as your ad becomes more targeted, the higher the click through rate would be ideal.

In the split test process, try out popular beliefs with scientific backings such as women react favorably if the color pink is dominant on your ads, and though it may not be entirely true for all women, at least a majority of them would be a considerably commanding number if you think in terms of buying power.

And there is only one way to find out and that is through split testing.

FACEBOOK AD SPLIT TESTING; HOW TO DO IT?

Are you a typical "set it and forget it" Facebook advertiser? What's typical? Well, maybe you've launched an ad campaign, let it run, and been disappointed with the results.

Maybe you've gotten too few clicks for too high a cost. Maybe, you've thrown your hands in the air in anger and frustration, cursing Facebook's ad platform and swearing to never spend another dime with them.

Sound farfetched? The reality is, it happens every day to businesses all over the world who advertise on Facebook.

So if you are ready to give Facebook another chance and willing to learn few simple tips to ensure success the next time, read on.

First of all, Facebook is not to blame. You're the one who creates the ads, determines who your target audience is, and is responsible for monitoring and tweaking your ads to maximize success.

MONITORING AND TWEAKING?

That's right, unlike running an ad in your weekly or monthly newspaper, Facebook gives you access to results that are about as "real time" as it gets.

The advantage here is that you can actually run multiple ads simultaneously to a variety of target audiences and then identify the winners and stop running the losers.

The bottom line is that you simply need to test, test, test, and tweak, tweak, tweak. And it takes a tiny budget and a short amount of time to do. Say you're going to run an ad. You'll first want to identify an image that will attract attention before your prospects even look at the ad's headline.

How do you know what image to use? It's easily accomplished by "split testing." And Facebook actually provides you with the tools to make this pretty simple. Each ad that you run can include multiple images.

After you've found the one that resonates with your audience (I.e. it gets more clicks than the other), move on to split testing another variable, like your headline or description text.

Overall, there are not all that many things you have the ability to change inside your Facebook ads, but here is a list of the four general areas where you have the ability to test and improve:

1.   Your Image - Remember, an image is not always just about the picture. It could be background color or even the size or perspective of the image's contents. It may even be the text you include as part of your image.

2.   Your Copy - Is your message clear? Does it grab your target audience's attention? Is it relevant to them? Try changing your ad copy or even what it is you are asking your audience to do.

3.   Your Target Audience's Interest - Facebook targeting can be infinitely tweaked when it comes to audience interest. Is your interest, set too broad? Is it relevant to the message you are communicating? Does the interest suggest that your target is even going to buy what you are selling? Remember that someone who likes "drinking wine" may not be the same as someone who likes "Napa Valley AVA."

4.   Your Target Audience's Demographics - Try splitting your audience down into age, gender, etc. and then try your ads. The better you do this the better your ads should perform.

Note: Successful advertising inherently involves testing, and Facebook provides one of the simplest, quickest, and most targeted ways of ensuring your success.

WAYS TO SPLIT TEST YOUR PPC CAMPAIGNS

Pay per click advertising has become a very popular marketing tactic used by businesses to promote their services and products. Without the proper campaign management and testing, you can end up spending a lot of more money in the long run.

That is why I want to show you just a few things you can do to better increase your ROI with your PPC marketing campaign.

Things to test within your PPC campaign to not only see which works better for you, but also save you much needed money in the long run.

1.   Ad titles: Make sure you create multiple ads within your campaign, never use just one ad and expect to see great results. Using different ad titles will tell you which one is attracting more viewers to click on the ad. You can see these results by looking at the impressions you are receiving from a number of clicks you are gaining. This is your standard CTR (click through ratio). The more catchy the ad title is, the more prone a user is to click on your ad.

2.   Ad descriptions: To go along with your multiple ads, you will need to create multiple descriptions for each. This is the text that will be displayed under your ad title and will make or break you from receiving a click or the users passing your ad by for the next.

Do not promise things that your site cannot deliver on, that will result in wasted money as the viewer will leave the site once they see it is not what they were searching for.

3.   Time of day: Test your ads at different times of the day and night, you may find what you are advertising for will work best late at night instead of early in the morning.

If you are on a limited budget, this is something you must be doing. Why set up your campaign to run 24 hours when your best traffic comes between 10 am - 5 pm? You can see within your campaign and website stats which times of day are producing better than others.

4.   Landing pages: This is often overlooked by many as new users to pay per click marketing will simply send the viewer straight to the home page of their website.

I highly recommend setting up an actual landing page that gives the users just enough information on the key phrase they searched for yet not giving them full access to other pages of your site. In the end, you either want them to buy something or fill out a form. So give them just that on your landing page and maybe some contact information, privacy policy and any terms they may need to know.

To take this a step further, set up multiple landing pages and see which one is converting the best for you. If you are only using one landing page, you will never know how much better you could be doing unless you built a few of them and tested them against one another.

5.   Location targeting: Look at your website stats and see which states and or cities are converting better for your website. You can then focus your PPC campaign to just those states or specific cities to really zero in on more business for your website.

Why spend money marketing to people in Houston who are not converting when you could focus on say Dallas who is converting. With these basic tips, you can be on your way to seeing a better ROI for your pay per click marketing campaigns.

Without split testing, you are blind to knowing what will work best for your website and in the end, bring in more clicks that convert.

According to what we just said, there is a really fast way to create multiple ads literally in few seconds (because facebook does not do it), and it is Qwaya. It looks similar to Facebook Ads interface and with just one click creates multiple ads "mixing" headline, text, images which you can run on your facebook advertising platform.

CHAPTER 11: GET BETTER RESULTS SPYING COMPETITORS

Making money with your own market is quite a simple thing to do if you know how to make it work. But one thing that most of us do not know is the fact that there's more to just focus on your site alone.

If you think that it's just all about doing master techniques on your site alone to make a profit, well you are wrong. There's something else that you need to do that this chapter will briefly discuss with you.

Spying on a competition, this in itself explains it all. When you get into internet marketing, you also need to look into the fact that you are not the only one who is trying to get people's attention to what they are selling and offering them; there are a lot more out there who are just like you are trying to make more money. That is why it is very important to see what others are doing.

To find out what the other competitors are doing, all you need to do is follow these few very simple steps. First, go to Google and search the certain keyword of your market.

After that, you will see what people are bidding on and if anyone's bidding on the certain term of your choice. Next, check out the sites that come up with the results and see if there's any Adsense or any type of ads in it.

There are tools that you can use to see what people are bidding on, what keywords they are using, what their keywords list is, how much they are paying and how long have they been running. Use these effective tools in order to find the answer to the certain questions.

To find out what's working, figure out what you can do and how you can do better so that you will make your way to making a fortune.

HOW TO SPY ON YOUR COMPETITORS ADWORDS CAMPAIGNS

Adwords campaigns are tricky enough as it is but grows ever more complicated when you throw in the effect of solid competitors. It's extremely important to know what your competitors are bidding on, how much they are paying, and how those keywords are performing.

Lucky for you, Traffic Travis has among its many tools a method of spying on your competitors' AdWords campaigns, giving you a ton of useful data to build your own campaign.

TRAFFIC TRAVIS FOR ADWORDS SPYING

To get started, go to the PPC Analysis page and either load up an existing project if you have already done some keyword research in Traffic Travis. Always remember to save your keywords to TXT files so that you can load them up later as projects in other parts of the software.

If you don't have a project already created, add a new one with the "Add Project" button. Choose the name of your project, the version of Google to use for your research and then add your keywords under the keyword tab.

Again, if you have a TXT file already, load it up now. If not, create a list of keywords to look up.

I recommend keeping it relatively short each time so that you can analyze the data that shows up. If you have 2,000 keywords off the bat, it would take hours to sort through it all.

Once you've added keywords, create your project and then click on the "Start Update" button that appears on the PPC Analysis page. This will go through Google's AdWords listings and create a list of data to draw from regarding your keywords.

1.   Keywords: The Keywords tab will show the keywords along with how many ads are currently showing, and how many advertisers are rotating through these keywords. This is important to gauge competitor volume.

2.   Top sites: You can then look at the top sites for each keyword, allowing you to see where they show up, their average rank, and their overall listing strength in Google. This helps you see if Organic SEO might be a better route than PPC. Click on any top site to see the words that match your PPC list.

3.   Popular keywords: On this tab, you can see the maximum ads, minimum ads, and unique ads numbers. You can also see how many sites appear for each keyword, showing you which ones are the most popular based on the sites that were found.

4.   Website keywords: This last one will take those top sites and break them down to display, which keywords in your list they are optimized for. This will give you an idea of what kind of quality score they're enjoying, and how hard it would be to compete for those words organically. For the most

71

part, it may not seem like you're getting exact data about your competitors and their PPC campaigns, but if you take a close look, you actually gain a lot of information here.

You now know how many people have ads, how those ads rank, how well optimized they are organic.

HOW TO SPY ON THE PPC CAMPAIGN OF YOUR COMPETITOR?

PPC is a powerful way to generate targeted traffic to your website. If done right, you can earn a lot of money with it. However, in order to have a profitable campaign, you need to pick the right keywords. Otherwise, you will end up wasting a lot of money.

1.   Use the Google AdWords keyword tool. You are probably already familiar with this tool. In the AdWords tool, click on "Website Content" and enter your competitor's website address.

The AdWords tool will generate a list of keywords based on your competitor's website. It will also show you how competitive the keywords are.

2.   Use a PPC spy tool to find out what keywords your competitors are bidding on. With a PPC Spy tool, you can see all keywords each advertiser is bidding on, how much they are paying, how many clicks they are getting, and much more. You can also find out the real destination URL instead of the display URL.

With that feature, you can see if your competitor is actually tracking its pay per click campaigns.

If you find a profitable keyword that seems to be too expensive to bid on, check how difficult it is to get ranked on the first search engine results page. Sometimes it's better not get involved in the "bidding war" and simply try to get ranked naturally writing blog posts or articles.

If you want to use a PPC Spy tool, you might want to try a free one first and check the results before spending any money.

CONCLUSIONS

As a social media manager, understanding how to leverage Facebook Ads for your marketing strategy is essential.

Facebook Ads can transform your business social reach without hurting your budget. In this book, we share with you everything you need to know about advertising on Facebook—from setting up a campaign to tracking results.

Facebook advertising allows businesses to promote custom ads or content targeting a specific audience, with costs varying based on the reach and engagement the ad receives.

Facebook ads can appear in your target audience's News Feed or right column on Facebook. When you advertise on Facebook, you'll gain insight about your current and potential customers.

The data you collect through Facebook ads allows you to improve your ad targeting for a more efficient and effective advertising experience.

Above all, remember Facebook advertising best practices

Before you begin, remember these three Facebook advertising best practices:

1.   Always determine your objectives before you start. It's important to know the purpose of your Facebook Ad before you decide on a budget for advertisements. Understand whether the aim is to increase brand awareness, conversions, video views, etc.

Each action made by your audience on your Facebook ad costs money, so make sure you solidify your objectives before making those investments.

2.   Be specific to your audience targeting. Facebook houses millions, if not billions, of data points. Take the time to narrow your audience targeting to ensure your ad will appear where the people you want to see it will be.

Rotate your ads regularly. To avoid ad fatigue, rotate your Facebook ads regularly. 'Ad fatigue' is when people see your ad too many times, so they get bored and stop clicking.

Unfortunately, when your click through rate starts to drop, Facebook penalizes you, driving up your cost per click (CPC); which makes likes, comments, and click through more expensive. This affects both acquisition and engagement campaigns.

Finally, if you found this book useful in any way, a review on Amazon is always appreciated!

Thank you and good luck with Facebook Advertising!

www.ingramcontent.com/pod-product-compliance
Lightning Source LLC
Chambersburg PA
CBHW061200180526
45170CB00002B/896